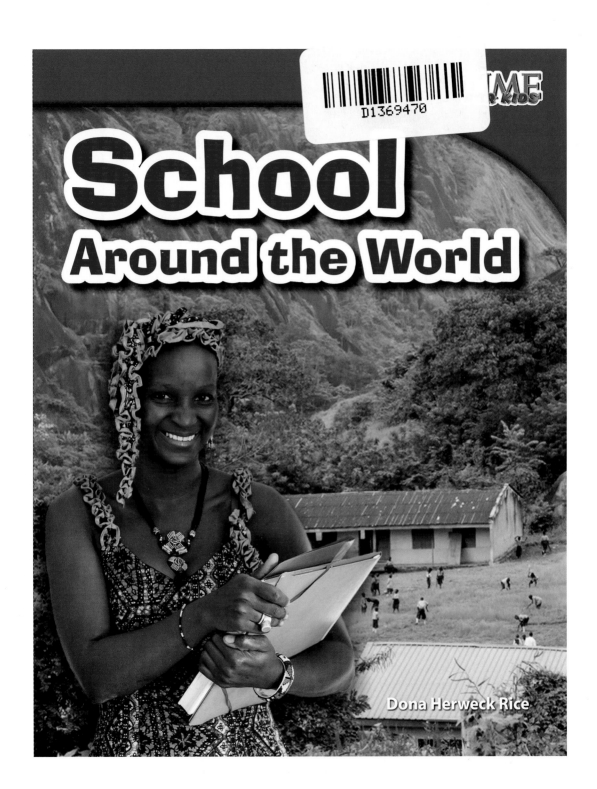

School
Around the World

Dona Herweck Rice

Dona Herweck Rice

Consultant

Timothy Rasinski, Ph.D.
Kent State University

Publishing Credits

Dona Herweck Rice, *Editor-in-Chief*

Robin Erickson, *Production Director*

Lee Aucoin, *Creative Director*

Conni Medina, M.A.Ed., *Editorial Director*

Jamey Acosta, *Editor*

Heidi Kellenberger, *Editor*

Lexa Hoang, *Designer*

Stephanie Reid, *Photo Editor*

Rachelle Cracchiolo, M.S.Ed., *Publisher*

Image Credits

Based on writing from *TIME For Kids.*

TIME For Kids and the *TIME For Kids* logo are registered trademarks of TIME Inc. Used under license.

Teacher Created Materials

5301 Oceanus Drive
Huntington Beach, CA 92649-1030
http://www.tcmpub.com

ISBN 978-1-4333-3654-6

© 2012 Teacher Created Materials, Inc.

Table of Contents

School Around the World 4

United States 8

Canada. 10

Australia 12

China 14

Mexico 16

Japan 18

Kenya. 20

Space School?. 22

On the Map. 24

Brrrng! 26

Glossary. 27

Index 28

School Around the World

Somewhere in the world right now, children are in school. Some adults are in school, too!

▼ a school in Africa

▲ a school in rural China

▼ a school in Thailand

From the time they are born, people start learning. School is a great place to do it.

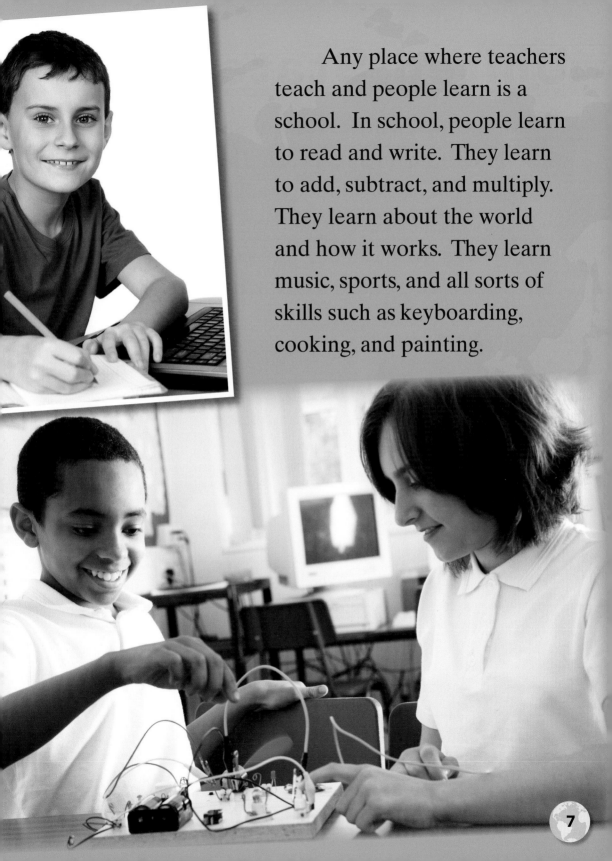

Any place where teachers teach and people learn is a school. In school, people learn to read and write. They learn to add, subtract, and multiply. They learn about the world and how it works. They learn music, sports, and all sorts of skills such as keyboarding, cooking, and painting.

United States

Most children in the United States begin school when they are about 5 years old. They go to school through high school and then **graduate** (GRAJ-oo-eyt) when they are 17 or 18. Sometimes, they go to **college** (KOL-ij) or a **trade school** after that. That is where they learn the skills they need to get a job.

Some children also go to special schools to learn things that are not taught in regular schools. They might go to a karate school or music school. Or, they might go to a school that teaches about **religion** (ri-LIJ-uhn) or **culture**.

All children in the United States must go to school. Sometimes their school is at home! These children are **homeschooled** by their parents or other friends and family.

This child is learning Jewish history and language at Hebrew school.

Canada

School in Canada is a lot like school in the United States. Five days a week, children get up in the morning and get ready for school. The school day starts in the morning and goes into the afternoon. Children study reading, writing, mathematics, science, and more.

There is one big difference. In Canada, there are two official **languages**. People speak English and French. Children learn both languages in school.

English	French
coffee	le café
juice	le jus
computer	l'ordinateur
office	le bureau

The French word for school is *école* (ey-KAWL).

Australia

School in Australia is a lot like school in the United States and Canada. Children study the same kinds of things. But some children live in the dry central part of Australia where not many people live. This area is called the outback. Children in the outback might go to school online. They listen to their teachers and send their work through a computer. This is called School of the Air.

It is no surprise which part of school is the favorite for most children around the world: recess!

▼ two aboriginal boys share a laptop

a bush school in the outback ▼

13

China

Children in China go to school, too. They study the same kinds of things that children study in other countries. But their school day is often longer. They also go to school six days a week instead of five. Their only day off is Sunday.

In China, children do not use letters to read and write. They use **characters**. Characters are like small pictures. Each character stands for a word. The characters are written in columns from the top down.

These are the Chinese characters for school:

学校

The children below are closing their eyes to think about how to solve a difficult problem.

Mexico

Children in Mexico must also go to school. But they only have to go from grades one through nine. Going to school is easiest to do in the large cities. Many small villages do not have schools. Children there do not always have a chance to earn an **education**.

In some places around the world, children earn letter grades for their work. An *A* is given for the best work. An *F* means failing. In Mexico, grades are given as numbers (1–10). A 10 is the best work. Zero to six is failing.

Children everywhere ➤ study hard and take pride in their work.

Japan

School in Japan can be hard work. Free play is not usually part of school. Children eat lunch in the classroom with their teacher. They also clean the classroom. The children wipe the desks and walls. They even sweep the floor.

School in Japan lasts most of the year, with one month off in the summer. In Japan, children are expected to work as hard as they can and learn many things well.

▼ A Japanese teacher and her students give thanks before eating lunch together.

A student sweeps the classroom. ▼

18

In Japan, the teacher is called the *sensei* (sen-sey).

Temporary classrooms were set up in a Miyagi gym after the March 2011 earthquake and tsunami damaged school buildings.

Kenya

In Kenya, many children walk to school. They must get up early to get to school on time. It is their job to arrive before the teacher does so they can get the classroom ready.

The students study many things. They even study **hygiene** (HAHY-jeen), or learning to keep themselves clean. They also study languages. Students may study three different languages in one day!

The school gives the students their lunch. Some students go home after lunch. Other students pay extra money to attend school after lunch.

eating lunch ▼

Children in Kenya may learn many languages, including Swahili, English, and French.

walking to school ➤

Space School?

Astronauts have traveled into space for many years. Some astronauts even live in space for long periods of time. They study the effects of space on living things, such as plants and people. Space is a kind of school for them.

▼ An astronaut studies the effects of gravity on plants.

▲ Could these be the school buses of the future?

Someday, whole **communities** may live in space. Then children might go to school in space. Maybe they will replace their backpacks with jet packs and fly to school! Children may even take a field trip to Mars! In the future, every class might be an adventure.

On the Map

Can you find all the places in this book?
Take a look!

Canada

United States

Mexico

China

Japan

Australia

Kenya

Brrrng!

Wherever you are in the world, chances are good that at the end of the school day, a bell rings. That sound tells you school is over for the day. Brrrng! Brrrng! Time to pack up your books and go home. Tomorrow will be a new day for learning. Goodbye!

Glossary

astronauts—people who travel into space

characters—symbols used in writing

college—a school of higher education for learning a profession or other advanced skills

communities—groups that live close together with a common government or other connection

culture—the ideas, knowledge, beliefs, customs, and practices of a group of people

education—knowledge learned through school

graduate—to receive a diploma after a course of study

homeschooled—when a child is taught at home by parents, family friends, or other family members

hygiene—self-care and cleanliness

languages—words and the ways they are used by groups of people

religion—a set of beliefs and practices around the cause and nature of the universe

trade school—school for learning an occupation, especially a craft

Index

aboriginal, 13

Africa, 4

Astronauts, 22

Australia, 12, 25

Canada, 10–12, 24

characters, 14–15

China, 5, 14, 25

college, 8

communities, 23

culture, 9

English, 11, 21

French, 11, 21

Hebrew school, 9

homeschool, 9

hygiene, 20

Japan, 18–19, 25

Jewish, 9

Kenya, 20–21, 25

languages, 11, 20–21

Mars, 23

Mexico, 16, 24

Miyagi, 19

outback, 12–13

religion, 9

School of the Air, 12

sensei, 19

space, 22–23

Swahili, 21

Thailand, 5

trade school, 8

United States, 8–10, 12, 24